Old Sturbridge Village

9 10 0940 11 10 09

Harcourt
SCHOOL PUBLISHERS

Visit *The Learning Site!* www.harcourtschool.com

Learning from the Past

Brothers Albert and Joel Wells liked history. In the 1920s, they collected things from the past. They learned a lot about history from these objects. They learned what people did, how they did it, and even why.

Albert Wells

In the 1830s, most people lived on farms. Albert was interested in farm technology. He collected tools. Joel collected many clocks and paperweights. The paperweights were made of glass. Inside were pretty things, like flowers.

Joel Wells

This tool was used on farms in the 1830s.

All of the clocks Joel collected had to be wound by hand.

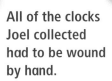

1830s stove from the Old Sturbridge Village collection

Albert collected many things. His wife, Ethel, was also a collector. They kept most of their collections in their house. But things got very crowded. Finally, there was little space left in the house.

Their son George wanted to open a museum. Then other people could see the collections. The museum would show all the things where they belonged. That place might be a farm, a home, or a shop. The museum would help people understand what life was like long ago.

A Living Museum

The family started looking for land. Much of the museum would have to be outside. The Wells family decided to build a whole village. It would have all of the things that an 1830s village had. It would show all of the things that the Wells family had collected.

They found the right piece of land in Sturbridge, Massachusetts. In the 1830s, many people had farmed on that land. A few of the old buildings were still there.

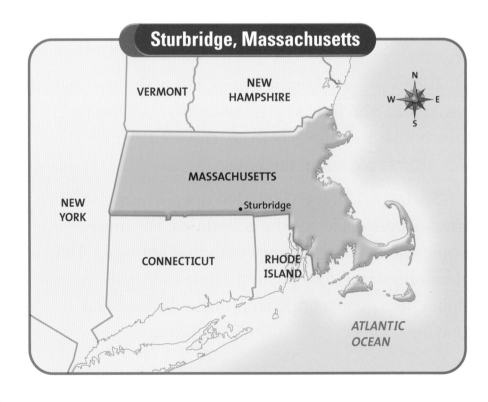

Sturbridge, Massachusetts

VERMONT

NEW HAMPSHIRE

N
W — E
S

MASSACHUSETTS

NEW YORK

•Sturbridge

CONNECTICUT

RHODE ISLAND

ATLANTIC OCEAN

This shows how a village might have looked in the 1800s.

Learning from the Past

The land had once belonged to the Wight family. In about 1789, Oliver Wight built a house on the land. He and his wife lived there for a while. In the early 1800s, the house was made into an inn. People could eat and sleep there.

Today, people can again stay overnight at the Oliver Wight House.

In 1863, Oliver's great-nephew George Wight bought the house. That house was still standing when the Wells brothers bought the land.

Moving Days

The Wells family needed more buildings. They decided to buy them. Then those buildings would be moved to Sturbridge.

They wanted the buildings to be like 1830s buildings. The family looked all over New England for houses and shops from that time.

They first bought a sawmill from Connecticut. Then came a barn from New York. Other buildings came from as far away as Maine.

These buildings were moved to Old Sturbridge Village.

Soon the land began to look like a village with homes and shops. These buildings would have been part of a real 1830s community.

Some buildings had to be made. But the builders followed old plans or copied real buildings. Sometimes they used wood that was saved from old buildings that were no longer standing.

At Home in the Village

In 1946, Old Sturbridge Village was ready to open. Visitors saw people doing things people did in the 1830s. The people doing them were like actors in a play. For a few hours every day, they played a role. They acted as if they did not know anything that happened after the 1830s.

Everything seemed real. Some people thought it was as if a time machine had taken them into the past.

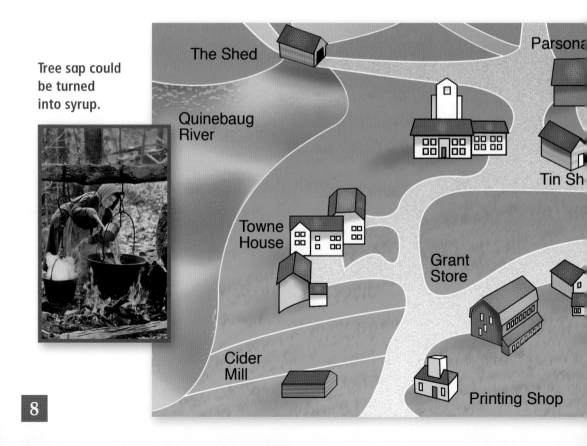

Tree sap could be turned into syrup.

The Shed

Parsona

Quinebaug River

Tin Sh

Towne House

Grant Store

Cider Mill

Printing Shop

Visitors still come to Old Sturbridge Village. There are more than 40 buildings in the village now. Visitors can go inside the houses. There, they find actors doing the work villagers did in the past. Women might be spinning wool. They might be working on a quilt.

The men might be making shoes or baskets. They might be building a fence for the cows and horses.

In one building, young visitors can dress in costumes and pretend they are living in the 1830s.

Women made their own wool.

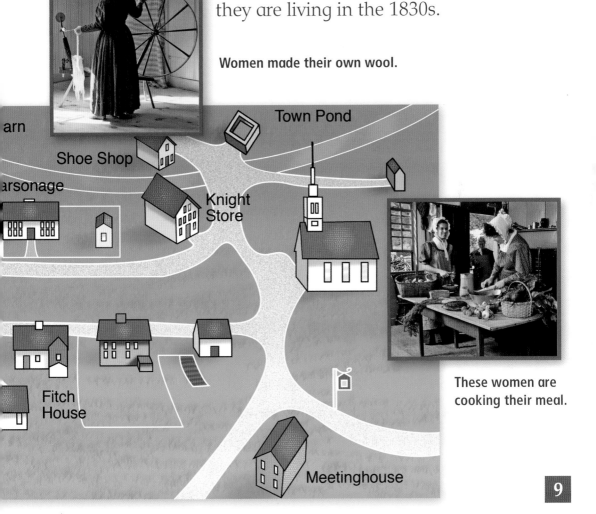

Town Pond

arn

Shoe Shop

arsonage

Knight Store

Fitch House

Meetinghouse

These women are cooking their meal.

Barns and Fields

Today, visitors to the village can see a working farm. They can learn what farming was like in the 1830s. Most farms then had more than one kind of crop. One field might have corn, and another field might have wheat. There would be other crops, too, like vegetables and pumpkins. The farmers sold these crops to other people.

Farm women grew food to eat in their kitchen gardens. They grew vegetables and herbs. They used the herbs to flavor food and to make medicines.

Girls helped their mothers with the work in the home and garden.

Every farm had animals. There were chickens and geese, pigs, sheep, and cows. Barn cats kept the mice away. And there was always at least one dog.

Young children helped out on the farm.

There were horses for riding or for pulling wagons or carriages. Oxen did the heavy jobs, like pulling up tree stumps and plowing fields. A few farmers had mules. For many years, cows were allowed to eat grass in the village green.

Visitors to the village can see farm animals in the fields or in a barn. They can also see horse-drawn carts and carriages on the village's roads.

Oxen were used for heavy work, such as pulling farm machinery.

Around the Village

People did not go far to shop in those days. A village would have many different kinds of shops. A wagon ride could take a family into the village to buy what they needed.

Maybe they stopped first at the bank to get money. Next, the family might go to the general store. If the farmer had vegetables in the wagon, he could trade them for something in the store. At the tin shop, the family could get things like pots, pans, and lamps.

People used lanterns to hold their home-made candles.

The Power of Water

The wheels that do the work in mills run on waterpower. Workers built a dam to hold back a river. Then they could use the water to power the mills.

The next stop might be at a cider mill. The farmer brought his baskets of apples there. The mill turned the apples into cider, which is like apple juice. The mill was run by waterpower.

Children spent their day in the one-room schoolhouse. They learned to read and write and to work with numbers.

Today, visitors can go to the bank, tinsmith, and other businesses. They can see the mill and the school. People can imagine what it was like to be a family in the 1830s.

In the schoolhouse, all the grades were in one room.

13

Visitors to the Past

Over the years, Old Sturbridge Village has changed. There are more buildings. There are special programs. But the idea that the Wells family had is the same.

The village is still a living museum. Everything in it is real. Visitors see the same things the early New Englanders saw. In Old Sturbridge Village, visitors get to do many things.

They can play with the same toys. They can wear the same clothes. They can hear the same sounds and smell the same smells. They can even taste the same food.

Games and Toys

Visitors can see children using real toys. They might see a little girl playing with a doll from the 1830s. A little boy might be pulling a painted wooden toy with wheels. Children who visit Old Sturbridge Village can even learn to play 1830s games.

People come from all over to visit the village. They learn what it was like in the past. They can visit the shoe shop or the printing shop, where books were made. They can see what life was like in the 1830s.

Visitors also learn about community. Everyone in a village knew everyone else. Neighbors helped neighbors. For a few hours, visitors can feel what life was like in the 1830s.

Visitors learn about the village by becoming part of it for a little while.

Think and Respond

1. What happened after the Wells family bought land in Sturbridge?

2. What are visitors likely to see when they go into an old house in the village?

3. What is a mill?

4. What can you learn about the past from studying objects?

5. Why might people want to work at Old Sturbridge Village?

 # Activity

Quilts are made from different pieces of cloth that have been sewn together. Use different materials to design a quilt. You might use construction paper or colorful ads from magazines to make your quilt.